DISESTABLISHMENT AND DISENDOWMENT: WITH A PROPOSAL FOR A REALLY NATIONAL CHURCH OF ENGLAND

(1873)

BY

ALFRED RUSSEL WALLACE

British Library Cataloguing-in-Publication Data
A catalogue record for this book is available from the
British Library

Alfred Russel Wallace

Alfred Russel Wallace was born on 8th January 1823 in the village of Llanbadoc, in Monmouthshire, Wales.

At the age of five, Wallace's family moved to Hertford where he later enrolled at Hertford Grammar School. He was educated there until financial difficulties forced his family to withdraw him in 1836. He then boarded with his older brother John before becoming an apprentice to his eldest brother, William, a surveyor. He worked for William for six years until the business declined due to difficult economic conditions.

After a brief period of unemployment, he was hired as a master at the Collegiate School in Leicester to teach drawing, map-making, and surveying. During this time he met the entomologist Henry Bates who inspired Wallace to begin collecting insects. He and bates continued exchanging letters after Wallace left teaching to pursue his surveying career. They corresponded on prominent works of the time such as Charles Darwin's *The Voyage of the Beagle* (1839) and Robert Chamber's *Vestiges of the Natural History of Creation* (1844).

Wallace was inspired by the travelling naturalists of the day and decided to begin his exploration career collecting specimens in the Amazon rainforest. He explored the Rio Negra for four years, making notes on the peoples and languages he encountered as well as the geography, flora, and fauna. On his return voyage his ship, Helen, caught fire and he and the crew were stranded for ten days before being picked up by the Jordeson, a brig travelling from Cuba to London. All of his specimens aboard Helen had been lost.

After a brief stay in England he embarked on a journey to the Malay Archipelago (now Singapore, Malaysia, and Indonesia). During this eight year period he collected more than 126,000 specimens, several thousand of which represented new species to science. While travelling, Wallace refined his thoughts about evolution and in 1858 he outlined his theory of natural selection in an article he sent to Charles Darwin. This was published in the same year along with Darwin's own theory. Wallace eventually published an account of his travels *The Malay Archipelago* in 1869, and it became one of the most popular books of scientific exploration in the 19th century.

Upon his return to England, in 1862, Wallace became a staunch defender of Darwin's landmark work *On the Origin of Species* (1859). He wrote responses to those critical of the theory of natural selection, including 'Remarks on the Rev. S. Haughton's Paper on the Bee's Cell, And on the Origin of Species' (1863) and 'Creation by Law' (1867). The former of these was particularly pleasing to Darwin. Wallace also published important papers such as 'The Origin of Human Races and the Antiquity of Man Deduced from the Theory of 'Natural Selection" (1864) and books, including the much cited *Darwinism* (1889).

Wallace made a huge contribution to the natural sciences and he will continue to be remembered as one of the key figures in the development of evolutionary theory.

Wallace died on 7th November 1913 at the age of 90. He is buried in a small cemetery at Broadstone, Dorset, England.

DISESTABLISHMENT AND DISENDOWMENT: WITH A PROPOSAL FOR A REALLY NATIONAL CHURCH OF ENGLAND

(1873)

The agitation now going on for disestablishment and disendowment of the English Church, calls for more notice than it has hitherto received from those who, while agreeing with the necessity for some such movement and the abstract justice of its main object, do not look upon the existing Established Church merely as a powerful rival sect, whose prestige and influence are to be diminished as soon as possible and at almost any sacrifice.

At the various meetings recently held in favour of disestablishment, none of the speakers appear to have said anything as to the details of the proposed or desired legislation; none have hinted at any practicable and beneficial mode of applying the national property now held by the Church, or of preserving and utilizing for national objects the parish churches and other ecclesiastical buildings spread so thickly over our land, and which constitute a picturesque and impressive record of much of our social and religious history for nearly a thousand years. The only thing we have to guide us as to the aims and objects of these agitators is a constant reference to recent legislation in the case of the Irish Church, and we are therefore left to infer that some very similar mode of dealing with the English Church, its property and its buildings, is what these gentlemen have in view. But if this be so, it is surely the duty of all who have the social and moral advancement of their country at heart, and are uninfluenced by sectarian rivalry, to protest against any such scheme as in the highest degree disastrous. It may be thought by many that this agitation cannot possibly succeed in gaining its object for a very long time, and that it is useless to discuss now what shall be done at some indefinite and distant future. But this may be altogether a mistake; gross abuses do not now live long, and when an agitation is begun as powerfully and influentially as this one, supported as it will undoubtedly be by the great mass of the operative class, and made a party cry at future elections, the end may not be far off. We may then find it too late to introduce new ideas, or to persuade the Nonconformist leaders of the movement to give up their special programme, however injurious some portions of that programme may be to the best interests of the country.

My object in this paper is, therefore, to urge upon all

independent liberal thinkers to lose no time in taking part in this movement, laying down at once certain principles to be adopted as an essential condition of securing their support; and I propose, further, to show a practicable mode of carrying out these principles so as to produce results in the highest degree beneficial to the whole community.

The main principle that should guide our action in this matter, I conceive to be--that existing Church Property of every kind is National Property, and that no portion of it must under any circumstances be alienated, either for the compensation of supposed or real vested interests, or to the uses of any sectarian body; and further, that the parish churches and other ecclesiastical buildings must on no account be given up, but be permanently retained, with the Church property, for analogous purposes to those for which they were primarily established--the moral and social advancement of the whole community.

That the property now held by the Established Church is national property, is generally admitted; and also that the Church, as represented by a body holding particular religious opinions, can have no permanent vested interest in that property, although the individuals of which it is composed may have life-interests; and the case of the Irish Church should be a warning to us to look far enough ahead, and prepare for the inevitable change so much in advance of any immediate political necessity for it that we may allow all individual vested interests to expire naturally, and so have no need to make special compensation for them. In Ireland every kind of vested interest was brought forward, and it was even claimed that, as every clergyman had a chance of obtaining a better living, or of becoming a bishop, he should be compensated accordingly; and that every member of the Church had an actual vested interest in its maintenance during his life. It was because all legislation had been put off till it could no longer be delayed, that these interests had to be considered, and the result was, that a sectarian Church was permanently endowed with a large amount of the national property. But any such necessity of compensation for vested interests of individuals may be obviated by a little foresight, and by legislating sufficiently early to allow everyone to retain his rights and privileges in the Church during his lifetime. All individual vested rights would thus be satisfied, and it is probable that they would not interfere with the complete establishment of a new system at a comparatively early period, because a transition state is always an unsatisfactory and an unpleasant one; and long before half the individual lives had expired, and perhaps in the course of a very few years, the change might be voluntarily and completely effected.

While legislation was proceeding in the case of the Irish Church, it was made sufficiently clear that it is almost impossible suddenly to abolish any such great national institution, and to find any suitable mode of applying the surplus property, without grievous waste, or so as to be really beneficial to the community; and it was therefore almost felt to be a means of getting out of a difficulty that every shadow of a vested interest should be fully compensated, and the inconveniently large amount to be disposed of reduced to manageable proportions. I believe, however, that in the case of England no such difficulty exists, and that the whole of the Church revenues may be applied in such a manner as,--Firstly, to retain all that is most useful in the organization of the existing Church of England; 2ndly, to extend its sphere of usefulness almost indefinitely; 3rdly, to remove all cause for the ill-feeling with which it is viewed by Nonconformists, and by the members of other religious bodies; and lastly, to create, without violent change, a great national institution, which shall always be up to the highest intellectual level of the age, and be a means by which the moral and social advancement of the whole nation shall be permanently helped forward. In order to show how these desirable results may be obtained, it is necessary first to say a few words as to the status of our existing clergy, and the important of the functions they fulfil.

The Church of England, as a religious body, owes much of its power and influence in society to its venerable antiquity; to its intimate association with our great Universities; to its venerable antiquity; to its intimate association with our great Universities; to its establishment by law and its position in the Legislature; and to its possession of the cathedrals and parish churches, which from time immemorial have been the visible embodiments of the religion of the country. The clergy of the Church of England owe their chief influence for good in their respective parishes to their connection with these permanent and often venerable buildings; to their being the official representatives of a law-established religion; to their being the recognized heads, either officially or by courtesy, of almost all local organizations for self-government; and, though last not least, to their social position, their intellectual culture, refined manners, and moral character. It must, I think, be admitted that an institution which provides for the residence in every parish of the kingdom of a permanent representative of the best morality and culture of the age--a man whose first duty it is to be the friend of all who are in trouble, who lives an unselfish life, devoting himself to the moral and physical improvement of the community, who is a welcome visitor to every house, who keeps free from all party strife and personal competition, and who, by his education and training, can efficiently promote all sanitary measures and healthful amusements, and show by his example the beauty of a true and virtuous life--that an institution which should really do this, would constitute an educational machinery, whose influence on the true advancement of society can hardly be exaggerated. But in order that such an organization should produce the full beneficial effect of which it is capable, it is above all things essential that it should keep itself free from sectarian teaching, and from everything calculated to excite religious prejudices. So long as there is but one religious creed in a country, or as the dissentients form a small and uninfluential minority, the ordinary clergy may possibly effect much of the good here indicated; but with us this has become impossible, owing to the adoption of a fixed creed by the Established Church, and to the multitude of opposing sects, equal in political influence, and perhaps superior in the number and enthusiasm of their adherents. The earnest Nonconformist cannot look with satisfaction on a man who is unjustly paid by the nation to teach doctrines which he firmly believes to be erroneous; while the conscientious and well-informed sceptic can hardly respect one who is not only often inferior to himself in mental capacity as well as in acquired knowledge; but who professes to believe and continues to teach as fact much that modern science has shown to be untrue. The clergyman, on the other hand, too often considers that every dissenting chapel in his parish is an evil, and looks upon every dissenting minister as an opponent.

The time seems now to have come when we shall have to get rid of the anomaly and the injustice of devoting an elaborate organization and vast revenues to sectarian religious teaching, while we loudly proclaim the principle of religious freedom in all our legislation. In order to get rid of an Established Church which is behind the age, there are men who would not hesitate to break up the whole institution, destroy or sell the churches, and devote the revenues to support free schools or hospitals. Such a step would, I believe, be an irreparable loss to the nation, and I propose now to consider what means can be adopted to preserve this great organized establishment, which has grown with the nation's growth, and has from time immemorial formed an essential part of the body politic, and to separate from it everything that can impair its efficiency or check its healthy development. I claim for every Englishman a share in this great property, devoted by our ancestors to the relief of distress, the protection and advancement of the people, the example of morality and virtue, the teaching of the highest knowledge of the age, and the inculcation of doctrines which were once universally accepted as absolute truths of the first importance for the welfare of mankind. I claim that it shall be preserved to our successors for analogous purposes, and that it shall be freed from association with all sectarian teaching, and from everything that can impair its value. Let it be reformed, not destroyed.

I will now proceed to show how it can be so reformed, and how it may be made a means of national advancement more efficient than all ordinary educational machinery, because its sphere of action will be wider, and because it will carry on a higher education than that imparted by schools, not for a few years only, but throughout the entire life of all who choose to profit by it. I will first sketch out what I consider should be the status and duties of the man who will take the place of the existing clergyman as the head and representative in every parish or district of the National Church.

First, as to his designation; he might be termed the Rector, a name to which we are already accustomed, and which does not necessarily imply a religious teacher. He should be chosen, primarily, for moral, intellectual, and social qualities, of a much higher character than are now expected. Temper and disposition would be carefully considered, as his usefulness would be greatly impaired if he were not able to gain the confidence, sympathy, and friendship of his parishioners. His moral character should be unexceptionable. He should be specially trained in the laws of health and their practical application, and in the principles of the most advanced political and social economy. His religion should be quite free from sectarian prejudices, but his private opinions on religious matters would be no subject for inquiry. He should, however, be of a religious frame of mind, so as to be able to work sympathetically with the clergy of the various religious bodies in his district, and excite in them neither distrust nor antagonism. He must have a fair knowledge of physiology, and of simple medicine and surgery, of the rudiments of law and legal procedure, of the principles of scientific agriculture, and of the natural-history sciences, as well as of whatever is considered essential to the education of a cultivated man. He should not be allowed to undertake the care of a parish till thirty years of age, and only after having assisted some rector in parish duties for at least five years.

The duties of the parish rector would comprise, among others, all those of the existing clergyman, *but he would never conduct religious services of any kind.* The parish church, with its appurtenances, would however be under his entire authority, in trust for the whole body of parishioners, to be used for religious services by all or any duly organized religious bodies, under such arrangements as he might find to be most convenient for all. Any religious body should be able to claim the use of the church as a right (subject to the equal rights of other such bodies), the only condition being that it should possess a permanent organization, and that its ministers should be an educated class of men, coming up to a certain standard of intellectual culture and moral character. The State might properly refuse the use of the churches to those sects whose ministers are not specially trained or well-educated men, on the ground that the public teaching of religion among a civilized people is degraded by being placed in the hands of the illiterate, and that such teachers are likely to promote superstition and increase fanaticism.

The rector would himself lecture in the church on

moral, social, sanitary, historical, philosophical, or any other topics which he judged most suitable to the circumstances of his parishioners. He would also allow the church to be used during the week for any purpose not inconsistent with the main objects of his position, but always having regard to religious prejudices so long as they existed, his first duty being to promote harmony and good-will, and to gain any object he might think beneficial by persuasion rather than by an abrupt exercise of authority. His knowledge of law, and his position as *ex-officio* magistrate, would enable him to settle almost all the petty disputes among his parishioners, and so greatly diminish law-suits. He would be an *ex-officio* member of the School Board, and of the governing body of any other public educational institution in his district. It would be his duty to see that new legislative enactments were brought to the notice of the persons they chiefly affected, so that no one could offend through ignorance. He might, if he pleased, visit the sick, if his services were asked for, but this would be altogether voluntary. It would be an essential part of his duty to be on good terms with the ministers of all religious sects in his district, to bring them into friendly relations with each other, and to induce them to work harmoniously together for moral and educational objects.

With a sphere of action such as is here sketched out, the rector of a parish would have far more influence for good than the existing clergyman can possibly have. The position would be one of weight and dignity, and would be, I believe, in a high degree attractive to some of the best men in the country. The choice of men to fill it would be indefinitely wider than it is now, since no special religious beliefs would be insisted on. The educational qualification being at once broad and high, and the appointment offering a wide field for useful labour, a sphere would be opened for a class of able men who, while they are imbued with the purest spirit of philanthropy, are too conscientious to teach religious doctrines they cannot themselves accept.

Some years ago, a proposal for a nationalization of the Church of England was made by Lord Amberley, in two very striking articles in the *Fortnightly Review*. These attracted much attention at the time, but do not seem to have produced any permanent impression. That proposal contemplated, if I remember rightly, perfect freedom of doctrine in the Church of England, and some power of modifying the formularies, while retaining the duty of conducting religious service, and of peaching as at present. It was probably felt that the difficulties of carrying out any such scheme were insuperable, and the advantages doubtful, since it involved some form of election or veto by the majority of the parishioners, or some mode of getting rid of a clergyman whose doctrines were greatly disliked. The Church would thus remain as sectarian as ever, but it would be a varying instead of a uniform sectarianism; and the necessary uncertainty of tenure would at once diminish the clergyman's influence for good, and render it more difficult to induce the best men to undertake the duties.

It seems to me to be an important and valuable feature of my plan, that it renders the rector's tenure of office for life almost certain, since the only causes (other than voluntary retirement) for his displacement would be immorality, or the fact of his making himself generally disliked by his parishioners. But the careful education and selection of the candidates, and the perfect freedom in the choice of the profession, would render either of these events of very rare occurrence. No man, who held any special doctrinal tenets so strongly as to make him intolerant of others, would choose a profession in which he would be compelled to recognize and work harmoniously with the clergy of all denominations; nor would one who felt himself by nature unfitted to associate familiarly with all classes, and make himself their friend and counsellor, undertake an office in which it would be his chief duty to do this. We may fairly anticipate, then, that our rectors of the future would be of as high a character as our judges are now, and that there would be as little necessity for the retirement of the one from his honourable duties as there is for the other. This would induce better men to seek the office, and would render them far more capable of effecting beneficial results than if they were mere temporary occupants, liable to be ejected by the votes of a majority of parochial schismatics.

If no hasty and irretrievable step is taken, there seems no reason why the change from the existing state of things to something like that here sketched out, might not be gradually effected without any interference with vested interests. The new rectors would take their places wherever vacancies occur, after the expiration of the time allowed for the disestablished Church to reorganize itself; and there need be no interference with the right of presentation to livings, the desirability of which, as positions of social importance, would be increased by the new arrangements. Some official recognition of the appointment would be required, and the stringency of the qualifications, both as to education and character, would render any abuse of this kind of patronage impossible. It seems highly probable that many clergymen who feel their present position more or less irksome, owing to their being obliged to read and teach much that they cannot accept as truth, would gladly resign their positions as ministers of a disestablished Church in exchange for that of rector in the National Church. Such men would be quite at home in their new position, for the wider duties of which many of them would be admirably qualified. Of course there would have to be some high officers fulfilling the duties of bishops, or inspectors over the rectors; and over the whole a Supreme Board, or a Minister of Public Instruction; but these are matters which would offer no difficulty in an institution of which the main features are so well marked out.

It has now, I trust, been shown that it would be possible to remodel the framework and machinery of the Church of England as by law established, so that it should become, in connection with the various voluntary religious bodies--which, while retaining their perfect freedom of action would be to some extent associated with it--a real and highly efficient National Church; and further, that this could be done without infringing any existing rights, while it would, on the other hand, confer on every section of the community the right, from which they have long been debarred, of an equal share in the use of national buildings, and in all the benefits that may be derived from a proper application of the national property. It now remains to answer, in anticipation, a few of the more obvious objections that may be made to this proposal; to discuss briefly a few important details; and to point out some of the advantages that would almost certainly result from its adoption.

The first objection that will probably occur, is a financial one. It will be asked how the existing endowments of the Church can be increased so as to make the position of Rector worth the acceptance of men of the required high standard of ability? The answer to this is to be found in the fact of the excessive inequality, both as regards area and population, of our parishes. In the north of England they are said to average six or seven times the size of those in the south, and we shall find that more than half of the parishes in England and Wales are far too small to require the exclusive services of a rector. A judicious system of union of small parishes, and approximate equalization of endowments, will entirely overcome the financial difficulty. A few facts and figures will make this plain. Some thousands of parishes have an area of from 5,000 to 12,000 acres, and even the largest of these are not too extensive for the supervision of an active and energetic man, while those of 4,000 or 5,000 acres and an average rural population would be comparatively easy work. But an examination of about 200 parishes, taken alphabetically in two series, shows that there are, as nearly as possible, one-half of our parishes which do not exceed 2,000 acres and have less than 1,000 population, the average population of these being less than 400 by the last census. Of the thirteen thousand parishes or places in England and Wales which form distinct ecclesiastical benefices, no less than 62 or 63 per cent. have under a thousand inhabitants. The average value of all the benefices is about 307*l.* a year, but this value is by no means in proportion to area or population, for the average of those parishes whose population is under 1,000 is still about 275*l.* a year.

A careful examination of the circumstances of these parishes, as regards area, means of communication, and increasing or decreasing population, would enable us to combine them, so that the number of rectors required would be little more than one-half that of the existing incumbents. About one-fourth of the parishes whose population is less than a thousand could most likely be attached to others with a population somewhat exceeding that number, while the remainder might be formed into groups of two, three, or four parishes. This would result in a total reduction of about 45 per cent. A further reduction might be made in towns, where three or four parish churches might almost always be placed under the control of one rector, because, although the population might be large, many of the duties he would have to fulfil in rural districts would be performed by existing establishments, such as corporations, mechanics' and other institutions, and ministers of religion; and his chief duties would be to protect and preserve the churches for the use of the various religious bodies, and to promote harmonious action among them. The average endowment might thus be nearly doubled, and in addition there would be the vacant parsonages and glebes, the rents of which might form part of the income of the rector of two or more combined parishes. We thus arrive at a nominal average endowment of about 600*l.* a year, while the actual inequalities are enormous; and we have to deal with a large number of advowsons which are private property fully recognized by the law. But this need not interfere with an approximate equalization of livings. Just as in other cases of far less momentous reforms, land or house property has to be given up for public uses, the owners receiving just compensation, so must the owners receiving just compensation, so must the owners of advowsons be dealt with. In cases of the union of parishes, the several patrons might either exercise their right of nomination jointly or alternately, or one might pay a sum to the other for exclusive possession. If they failed to agree to either of these alternatives, the joint advowson must be sold by public auction and the proceeds equitably divided between them. Equalizations of endowments might be treated on a similar principle. In every case they might be effected by taking a definite sum, say 100*l.* per annum, from one living and adding the same amount to another. The owner of the advowson which is increased in value might either pay a sum, to be determined by arbitrators, to the owner of that which is diminished, or the advowson which is increased must be sold, and the proceeds divided equitably as before. It would be advisable to leave some inequalities in the value of rectories, and while none should be under 300*l.* or 400*l.* a year, a few might remain as high as 1,000*l.* in important districts, to which men of special abilities would alone be appointed. The revenues now devoted to episcopal and cathedral establishments have not been reckoned as sources of increased rectorial incomes, although, whatever system of supervision might be adopted, it is probable that a considerable surplus from these revenues would remain.

It may, perhaps, be further objected, that the country

could not supply six or seven thousand men of the requisite ability and character, in addition to the clergy of the disestablished Church, who would continue in existence as an independent body. But we must consider that the new men would be only required in gradual succession as livings became vacant; and, as it is almost certain that no voluntary establishment would be able to appoint resident clergy in the thousands of small parishes with a very scanty population, the total number of educated men required for the service of the Church would not perhaps be very much greater than at present.

Although the power of nominating rectors now possessed by private persons is not proposed to be interfered with, candidates would have to pass a much more rigid examination, and to furnish much better evidence of temper and moral character, than is now required; and they would further have to submit to the probation of five years' service under a rector, which would sufficiently test their capacity and suitability for the office. All livings now in the gift of Government or of public bodies should be thrown open to public competition by annual examinations, the details of which need not now be considered.

It will doubtless be further objected, that the scheme now advocated is Utopian, and aims at an ideal perfection which could not be realized even were public opinion ripe for any such revolution; and also, that it will be repulsive to the feelings of a large number of persons by placing religion and religious teachers in a subordinate position. To this I would reply, that a few years ago, before the Irish Church had been disestablished, and when Household Suffrage and the Ballot were still ideal propositions which our Parliament would hardly seriously discuss, any such proposal as the present one would have been thoroughly Utopian; but I cannot admit that it is so now. The body which has set up the cry for disestablishment and disendowment of the Church of England is a more powerful and a more united one than that which inaugurated any of the other great reforms; and the probabilities seem to me to be great that they will attain their object in less than a score of years. If so, it is not Utopian to discuss the subject in all its bearings; and although my scheme may aim at an ideal perfection which it is not in existing human nature perfectly to attain, the question to be considered is whether this ideal is a just, a true, and a noble one; if it is so, we shall assuredly do well to keep it in view, and so legislate as not to prevent our successors from ever attaining it. Neither do I believe that such a scheme can be in any way degrading to religion; it will, on the contrary, keep up a connection between religious teaching and the State, and by dealing out equal justice to all creeds, will go far to do away with that sectarian animosity which more than anything else really degrades religion. As knowledge and true civilization spread more widely, it is to be expected that religion will become more and more a personal matter, without necessarily losing any of its influence on the human mind; and an organization which provides for the diffusion of those moral and social teachings which are the highest product of the age, must necessarily aid in the development of that religion which is the truest reflex of man's higher nature.

It now remains only to point out a few of the advantages which would result from the adoption of the scheme here advocated.

It will be generally admitted, that, were the English Church to be disestablished and disendowed, the Church buildings to be devoted to sectarian or secular uses, and the Church property applied in almost any way that can be suggested (other than that here proposed), a void would be left in the social organization of the country that could not easily be filled up. The clergy of rival sects, all equal and equally without authority in the eye of the law, could not possibly fulfil the various social and moral functions even of the present Established Church, still less could they ever attain the standard of usefulness which could be easily reached by men in the position I have indicated in the Church of the future. What that standard might soon become it is not only difficult to exaggerate, but difficult even adequately to realize, because no institution equally well adapted to produce great results has ever before existed. If we were to say that its beneficial influence upon society would be equal to that produced by the whole of our best literature, many would at first think it an exaggerated estimate. But a little consideration would, I think, convince them that it is on the contrary far too low. For literature only reaches certain defined and very limited classes, consisting largely of men who least require the lessons it conveys, while the great mass of the population know no literature, or only that of the cheap newspaper; and the teachings of modern science and philosophy, as well as the instruction to be derived from history and biography, would be to many of them as startling as the revelation of an unknown world. Most of these would be reached by the National rectors, whose duty and pleasure it would be to convey to the minds of their parishioners, in interesting and instructive series of lectures, some idea of the beauties of literature, of the marvels of science, and of the instruction to be derived from the example of great and good men. Is it possible to foresee the ultimate effects of such teaching, as a supplement to our new system of National Education, carried out systematically, not in our great towns only, but in every country parish, not by the occasional visits of itinerant superficial lecturers, but continued week by week, year by year, and from one generation to another, by a body of the best educated, the most earnest, and the most practical teachers the country can produce?

Men of this stamp would be able to influence all classes

for good; they would aid in introducing the best methods of agriculture and of household economy; they would be the men to see that sanitary inspectors and School Board did their duty; they would take care that in their district no common lands were wrongfully enclosed, no public paths stopped up, and generally no injustice done to those who did not know, or could not enforce, their legal rights. Not coming into competition with any class of men, and not exciting any sectarian or religious animosity, the National rectors might be in our age all that the monks and abbots were in the best monastic days--and much more--respected by the rich, loved by the poor, feared by the evil-doer, centres of culture and of morality throughout the land; by their example, their teaching, and their assistance, helping on the higher civilization, and thus fulfilling the noblest function that can fall to the lot of any body of men.

But besides these direct benefits to society, which such an institution would be naturally expected to produce, there are others of hardly less value which would incidentally flow from it, and a few of these I should wish to touch upon. One of the results of the extreme competitive activity of modern life, and of the somewhat commercial character of most of our institutions, is, that there are exceedingly few positions open to men of high intellectual culture and scientific or literary tastes, such as will leave them sufficient leisure to devote themselves to original research in their favourite pursuits. But the position of a National parish rector would supply this want in the most complete manner. From their liberal education and special training, and the high intellectual standard required for the appointment, a large proportion of them would be men of exceptionally active and powerful minds. They would have a good elementary knowledge of modern science and philosophy. Their duties, though numerous, and in the highest degree important, would not, as a rule, be laborious, and would leave them a considerable amount of leisure--and leisure with such men necessarily implies occupation. Some would devote themselves to science, some to experimental agriculture or horticulture, some to history, philosophy, or other branches of literature; and we may fairly conclude, that from the body of six or seven thousand National Church Rectors, we should have a very large accession to our original thinkers and original workers--a class of men who not only reflect glory on their country, but more than any others help on the work of human progress.

It has been already suggested, that the rectors would be able to see that sanitary inspectors and School Boards did their duty; but I think we may go further, and say, that over a large portion of the rural districts no sanitary or educational legislation will be efficiently carried out till some such body of men is called into existence. Their value, too, can hardly be exaggerated, as a means of obtaining trustworthy information on the working of any new law affecting our social relations, and especially those connected with pauperism. The narrow education, imperfect training, and sectarian prejudices of so many of the clergy of the Established Church, prevent their opinions having much weight, either with the public at large or with the Government. But the National rectors would be in a very different position. Their education and special training would render them well fitted to consider such questions in all their bearings, and their perfect independence would give weight to their opinions; while their means of obtaining accurate information would be much greater than that of any visiting inspector, who can seldom detect abuses which can be temporarily concealed, or which only occasionally become prominent.

These are some of the incidental advantages (and many others might be adduced) that would follow the establishment throughout the country of such a body of men as has been indicated; but I lay no stress upon these as arguments for the proposed change, compared with the direct and unparalleled advantage of establishing a truly National Church, in which every Englishman, whatever be his religious opinions, shall have an equal share; and of abolishing for ever, so far as it is possible to do so, all causes of local religious animosity. I would also claim a favourable consideration for this proposal, because it is a settlement of the question that would adapt itself to any possible future change in the religious beliefs of the community, and would therefore be permanent. Whether sects increased or diminished in number, and whether religion or secularism should ultimately prevail, an institution that should provide for the teaching of the best morality of the age to those most in need of such teaching, and that should aid in producing harmony and goodwill among all classes of society, would never become obsolete.

In conclusion, I would most earnestly press upon all unprejudiced thinkers, to consider the essential conditions of this great problem, not my imperfect exposition of it. Let them reflect that we are actually in possession of an elaborate organization, and an ample property, handed down to us by our forefathers, with whom it did at one time fulfil many of the high functions which I wish to restore to it. We have suffered it to remain in the hands of a narrow religious corporation, which in no sufficient degree represents either the most cultivated intelligence or the highest morality of our age, and which, by its dogmatic theology and resistance to progress, has become out of harmony both with the best and the least educated portion of the community. The question that now presses upon us is, shall we suffer this grand institution and these noble revenues to be irrevocably destroyed, or shall we bring them back to the fundamental purposes they were originally intended to fulfil, and which the conditions of modern society--its terrible contrasts of profuse wealth and grinding poverty, of the noblest intellectual achievements with the most degrading ignorance, of the most pure and elevated morality with the lowest depths of vice--render perhaps of more vital importance to our national well-being than at any previous epoch of our history?

Shall we preserve and re-create, in accordance with the principle of religious liberty, or shall we utterly abolish, our great historic National Church?

www.ingramcontent.com/pod-product-compliance
Lightning Source LLC
LaVergne TN
LVHW041239080426
835508LV00011B/1281